The Young Scientist Investigates

Seeds and Seedlings

by
Terry Jennings

CHILDRENS PRESS ®

CHICAGO

Library of Congress Cataloging-in-Publication Data

Jennings, Terry J.
    Seeds and seedlings / by Terry Jennings.
        p.   cm. — (The Young scientist investigates.)
    Includes index.
    Summary: Describes the seeds produced by different kinds of
plants, how they spread, germinate, and grow into a new plant.
Includes study questions, activities, and experiments.
    ISBN 0-516-08408-9
    1. Seeds—Juvenile literature. 2. Seeds—Experiments—
Juvenile literature. 3. Seedlings—Experiments—Juvenile
literature. [1. Seeds. 2. Seeds—Experiments. 3. Experiments.]
I. Title. II. Series: Jennings, Terry J. Young scientist investigates.
QK661.J46   1988
582'.0467—dc 19   88-22890
                                                                      CIP
                                                                      AC

North American edition published in 1989 by Regensteiner
Publishing Enterprises, Inc.

© Terry Jennings 1981
First published 1981 by Oxford University Press

Printed in the United States of America
1 2 3 4 5 6 7 8 9 10 R 98 97 96 95 94 93 92 91 90 89

Seeds and Seedlings

Contents

Flowers

Tulip

Bluebell

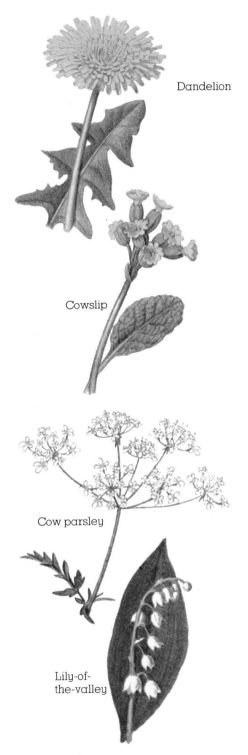

Dandelion

Cowslip

Cow parsley

Lily-of-the-valley

All seeds come from flowers. A flower is part of a plant. Some plants, such as tulips, have only one flower at the top of their stems. Other plants, such as bluebells, have more than one flower on each stem.

There are many different shapes and colors of flowers. Some are bright yellow like dandelions and cowslips. Some are white like cow parsley and lily-of-the-valley.

Many large trees have small flowers. They are often green. The flowers of grasses are also green. The flowers of rye grass, meadow grass and cocksfoot are green.

Sycamore

Elm

Ash

Rye grass

Meadow grass

Cocksfoot

Pollination

There are four parts to most flowers, arranged one inside the other. These are the sepals, the petals, the stamens, and the carpels.

The sepals protected the flower while it was a young bud. Many petals are brightly colored to attract insects to the flower. Many flowers also have scents so that bees and other insects will notice them and come to them.

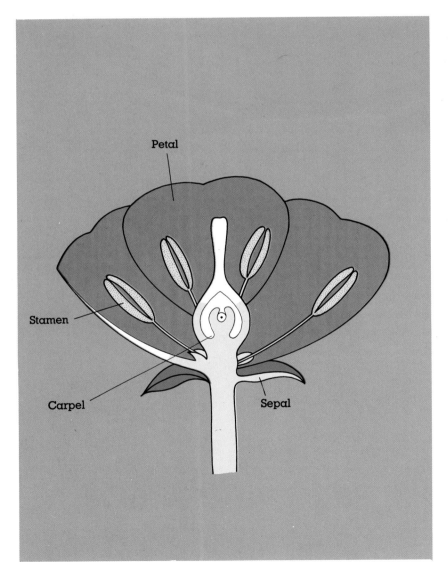

Petal

Stamen

Carpel

Sepal

Rose flower

The stamens make a yellow dust called pollen. If you shake a ripe flower, little clouds of pollen come off. When some pollen from the same kind of flower settles on the carpels, the carpels start to grow. Sometimes the pollen is carried to the carpels by bees and other kinds of insects. Sometimes the pollen is carried by the wind. Catkins have their pollen carried by the wind.

When the pollen settles on the carpels, the carpel grows to form a fruit. Some fruits contain just one seed. Other fruits contain many seeds.

Birch Catkins

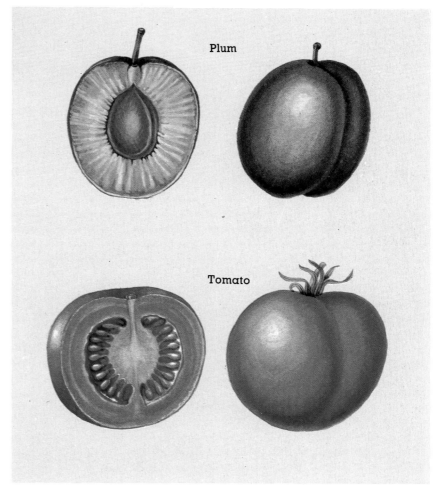

Plum

Tomato

Fruits and seeds

There are many kinds of fruits. The blackberry is a wild fruit. Every blackberry is made up of many little fruits. Each little fruit has a seed inside.

The fruit of the wild rose bush is called a hip. A hip is soft, red, and juicy on the outside. Inside these are several hard seeds.

Birds like to eat the soft parts of blackberries and hips. They do not like the seeds, though. The birds wipe the seeds off their beaks. Sometimes the birds swallow the seeds. But the seeds have a hard covering around them, and they pass through a bird's body without harm.

If the seeds reach good soil, they grow into a new plant. If all the seeds made by one plant were to fall on the same bit of ground they would not grow properly because the plants would be too close together. This means that the seeds need to be evenly scattered in order to grow.

Blackberry

Rose hip

6

Dandelion fruits

Dandelion seed

Dandelion plant

Dandelions grow almost everywhere. You can find them in the country and in cities. They flower from March to October.

The big yellow dandelion flower is made up of many tiny flowers. When the dandelion flowers die, white fluffy balls are left. People often call these white fluffy balls blowballs. They are really many tiny fruits.

Each fruit consists of a seed with its own little parachute. The wind blows the dandelion fruits to new places where they grow.

Tree fruits and seeds

An apple has a core. Inside the core there are brown seeds. From these seeds, new apple trees can grow.

The fruits of some other trees have wings so they can travel in the wind. If the seeds land in the right place, they can grow in the spring. Each fruit has one wing.

The sycamore tree fruits are pairs of seeds. Each seed has a curved wing. The wing twirls away in the wind like a helicopter.

In the fruit of the elm tree, each seed is surrounded by a thin oval wing.

Apple

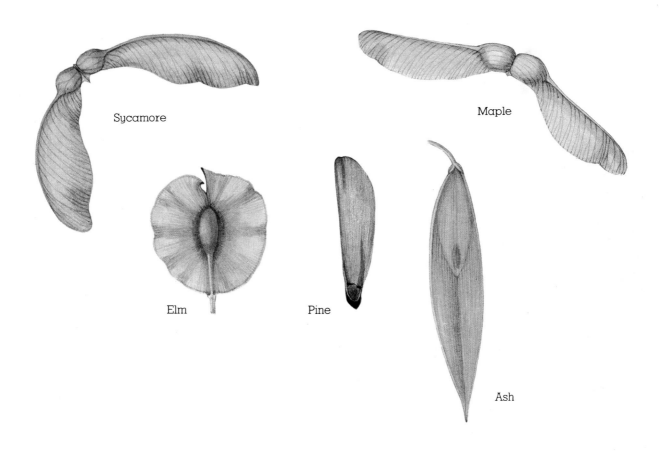

Sycamore

Maple

Elm

Pine

Ash

Seeds spread by animals

Wood Mouse

Gray Squirrel

Jay

Goosegrass   Burdock

Some fruits have hooks on them. These cling to the fur of animals or the clothes of people as they brush past. Goosegrass or cleavers has little green fruits that cling. The burdock fruits have hooks on them which catch onto an animal's fur or a person's clothes.

The seeds are often carried a long way. Then they are rubbed off, or they dry and fall off.

Some seeds are hidden in the ground by mice, squirrels, and jays. These creatures make little winter stores of fruits and nuts in the ground. They do not find them all again. Those that are left may grow.

More about spreading seeds

Poppy seeds are very small. They are scattered from little holes as the fruit stem sways in the wind.

Poppy seed head

Some fruits split open and the seeds fly out. The violet fruit splits into three parts and the seeds are thrown out.

Violet plant

Seed head

The yellow flowers of gorse and broom make a fruit called a pod. The white flowers of the pea plant also produce pods. When it dries, the ripe pod splits open with a loud pop. The seeds are shot out of the split pod. They may travel several yards.

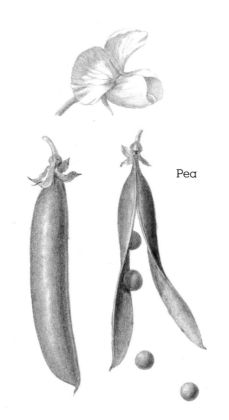

Pea

Gorse

The large fruits of the water lily float away on the water. When they settle in the mud, the seeds may grow into new water lily plants.

Water Lily

Do you remember?

(Look for the answers in the part of the book you have just been reading if you do not know them.)

1 Where do seeds come from?

2 What kinds of flowers do many large trees have?

3 How many parts are there to most flowers?

4 What task did the sepals do in the life of the flower?

5 What are two ways in which insects can be attracted to a flower?

6 What happens when pollen settles on the carpel?

7 How may pollen be carried to the carpel?

8 What is the fruit of the wild rose bush called?

9 What are the seeds of the wild rose bush like?

10 What happens when birds eat the seeds of soft fruits like those of blackberry and rose bushes?

11 Why do seeds need to be scattered?

12 How do dandelion seeds travel to a new place?

13 What is found in an apple core?

14 What are sycamore fruits like?

15 How are burdock seeds carried from the plant?

16 What happens when the fruit of the pea plant or broom bush ripens and dries out?

17 How are water lily fruits carried away from the plant?

Things to do

1 **Make a collection of dried fruits and seeds for your nature table.** Put a small index card with the name of the item against each fruit or seed.

2 **Make some winter decorations.** Dry some fruit or seed heads with the stems on. Wheat, oats, barley, poppies, wild grasses, hogweed and teasels are some that you might collect. Paint them and use them for decorations when flowers are not around.

3 **Make a wall display.** Collect packet fronts or labels of foods we eat which are kinds of seeds or fruits. Stick them all onto a large sheet of paper.

4 Make a list of fruits that are made into jam or marmalade. How many can you think of? You could illustrate your list with labels from the jars.

5 Make some model birds and animals from fruits and seeds. Collect some walnuts, acorns, and other fruits and seeds. Ask your teacher to help you make holes in them. Use matchsticks to put them together.

6 Make a seed collage. Draw a picture in pencil on a large sheet of paper. Glue seeds of different kinds onto the paper.

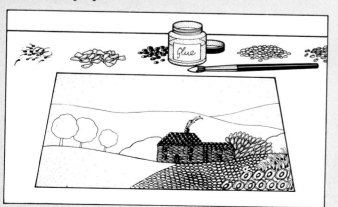

7 Write a story about a seed. Pretend you are a seed with hooks on it, such as a goosegrass or burdock seed. You get stuck on the fur of a dog. Describe what happens to you.

8 Find out about some berries found at Christmas time. Three kinds of berries thought of then are holly, ivy, and mistletoe. Discover all you can about these fruits and how they are scattered. Make a holiday card with a picture of all three fruits on it.

9 Use seeds to make musical instruments. Collect some empty metal and plastic containers, such as margarine tubs and cocoa tins. Put in seeds of different sizes to make musical instruments with them. The two empty halves of a coconut shell also make good musical instruments if tapped together. What does the sound remind you of?

Parts of a seed

Seeds are of all different sizes and shapes. But all seeds are alike in two ways. Every seed contains a tiny plant called an embryo. All seeds contain food that helps the embryo plant grow.

If you buy a packet of seeds from a shop, you will find that they are all hard and dry. The hard coat on the outside of the seed protects the embryo inside.

If you look closely at the seed you will find a little mark. This is a scar. The scar shows where the seed was joined to the inside of the fruit. On the hard seed coat you will also find a little hole. It is through this hole that moisture gets into the seed when it is planted.

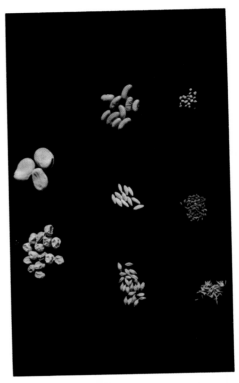

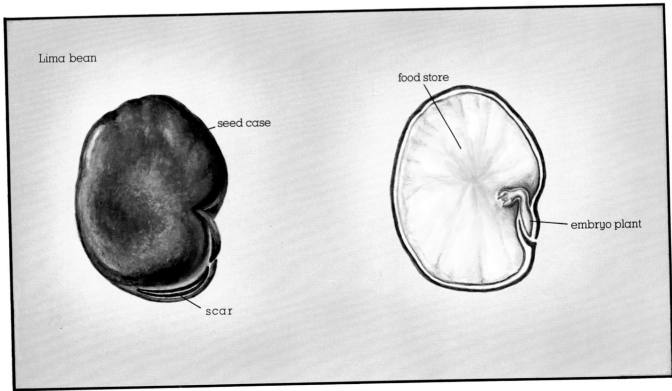

Lima bean

seed case

scar

food store

embryo plant

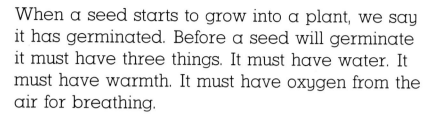

Germination

When a seed starts to grow into a plant, we say it has germinated. Before a seed will germinate it must have three things. It must have water. It must have warmth. It must have oxygen from the air for breathing.

The water comes from rain. The rain soaks into the soil. The warmth comes from sunshine. Sunshine warms the soil. The oxygen comes from the air which is trapped in little spaces between the pieces of soil.

If a seed has water and oxygen and is in warm soil, it will start to grow. A few seeds need to be in the dark before they will grow. But most seeds will grow in the light.

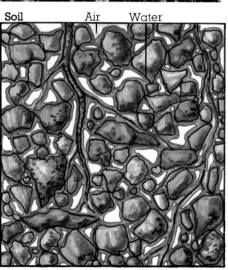

Soil   Air   Water

Roots

When a seed such as a lima bean is sown, the first thing that happens is that the seed swells. The seed swells as it takes in moisture. Then the embryo inside starts to grow. The skin of the seed splits and a little white root appears. The root thrusts its way down through the soil.

To protect the root from being damaged, its tip is covered with a soft, moist cap that slips easily between the pieces of soil. After a few days, tiny hairs grow out from the root. These tiny root hairs absorb water. Food called mineral salts is dissolved in the water. These salts come from the soil.

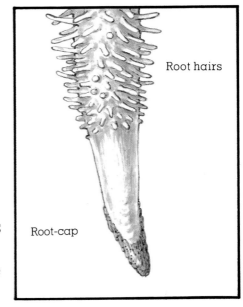

Root hairs

Root-cap

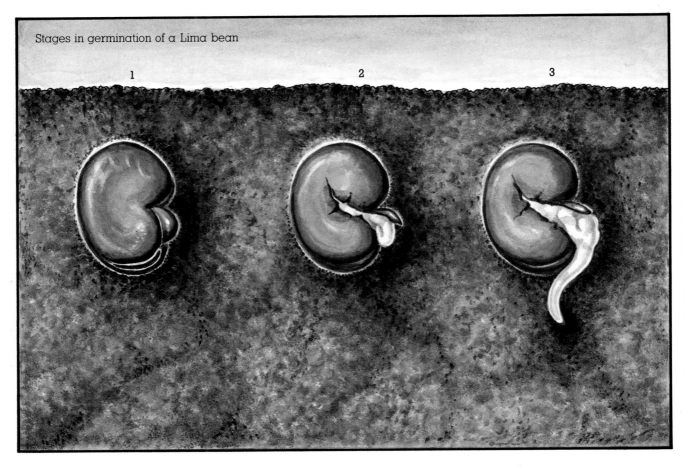

Stages in germination of a Lima bean

1   2   3

Shoots

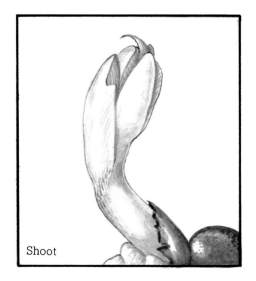

Shoot

Next a white shoot pushes upwards. When it is above ground, the shoot grows green leaves. Until this time the seedling has not been able to make any food for itself. It is fed by the two thick seed leaves that make up most of the inside of the seed. These seed leaves are packed with food from the parent plant.

After some time, many new leaves and roots are formed. We now have a small plant. There is a little bud at the top of the plant. This will go on growing.

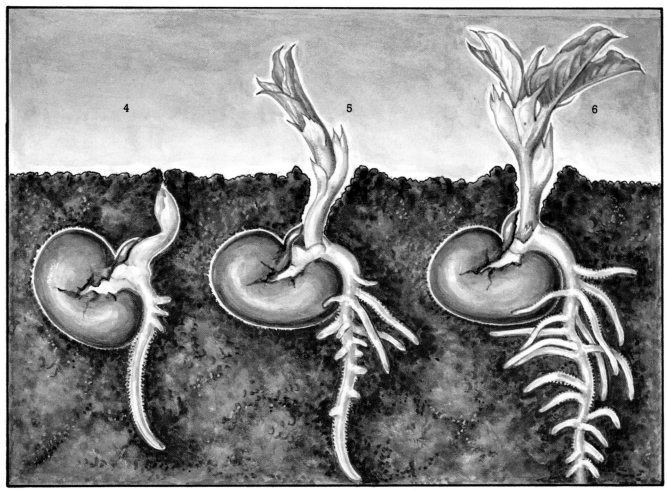

Food

In some seeds, such as mustard and cress, the little seed leaves get pushed up above the soil. The seed leaves open and turn green. Then they make food for the seedling. The leaves make food using the light of the sun, water, a gas called carbon dioxide from the air, and mineral salts from the soil.

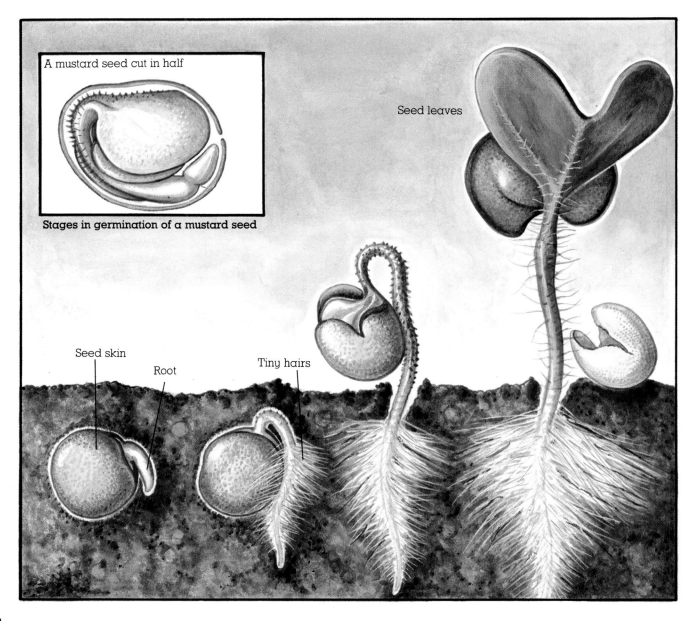

A mustard seed cut in half

Stages in germination of a mustard seed

Seed leaves

Seed skin

Root

Tiny hairs

Not all seeds carry their food in seed leaves. In some the food is stored around the embryo. The seeds or grains of corn or wheat, from which flour is made, store their food around the embryo. There is only one seed leaf. This is quite thin and is not packed with food. The seed leaf pushes to the surface and turns green.

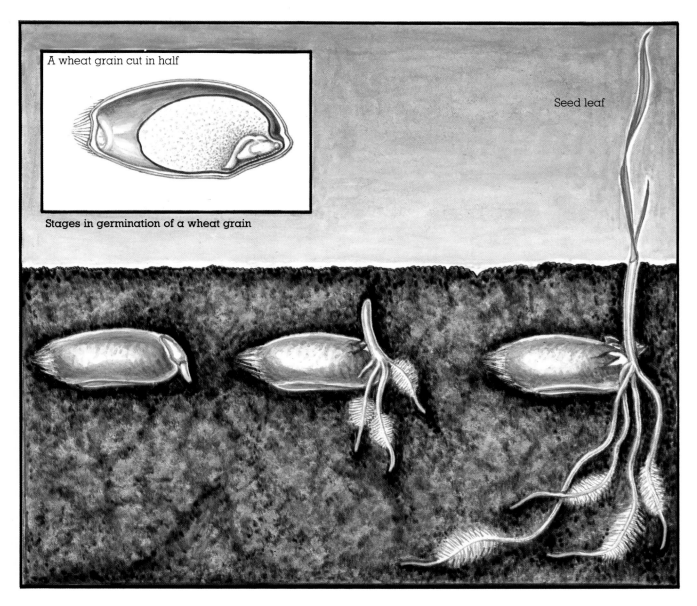

A wheat grain cut in half

Stages in germination of a wheat grain

Seed leaf

19

Seeds everywhere

Oak branch with acorns

Acorn

Young oak tree

Adult oak tree

Nearly all the plants around us – trees, shrubs, garden flowers, vegetables and even grass – started as seeds. The parent plants produced a lot of seeds. Some of the seeds grew into seedlings. Some of the seedlings grew into adult plants. Many of the seeds and seedlings died or were eaten. The adult plants produced more fruits and seeds.

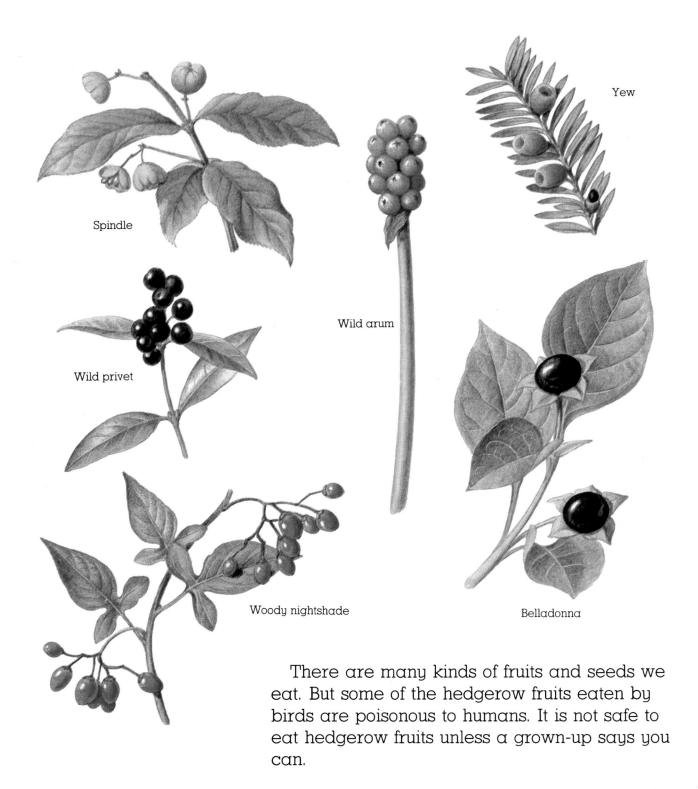

Spindle

Yew

Wild privet

Wild arum

Woody nightshade

Belladonna

There are many kinds of fruits and seeds we eat. But some of the hedgerow fruits eaten by birds are poisonous to humans. It is not safe to eat hedgerow fruits unless a grown-up says you can.

Cereals

Perhaps the most important plants in the world are grasses. Wheat, oats, and barley are all different kinds of grass. These food grasses are called cereals. Rye, corn, and rice are also cereals. The seeds of these cereals provide food for people all over the world.

The seeds of wheat, or wheat grains, are ground into flour. From flour we make bread and cakes. Oat grains are ground to make oatmeal. Beer malt is made from barley. And cornflakes are made from the grains of corn.

Harvesting wheat with a combine harvester

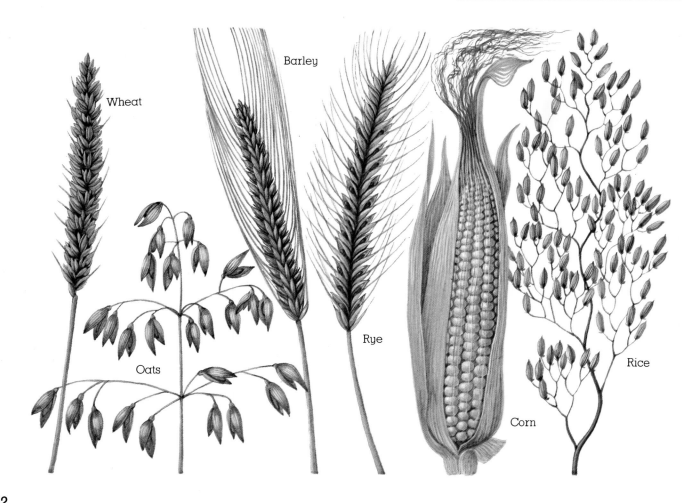

Wheat

Barley

Oats

Rye

Corn

Rice

22

Grasses

Grasses provide food for many of the animals that give us meat. Cows and sheep like to eat grass very much.

Grasses are important in another way. Growing almost everywhere, grass stops the soil from being washed away when it rains on hillsides and steep slopes.

Grass seeds are very light and easily blown around by the wind. When any bare patch of soil is left, grass seeds soon find their way there. The grasses grow quickly and cover the ground. Then the soil cannot wash away when it rains.

Planting seeds

We buy seeds in packets for our gardens. The seeds for gardens are specially grown in a nursery. The flowers or vegetables in the nursery are left until they have produced seeds. Then the ripe seeds are gathered. The seeds are put in the brightly colored packets ready for us to buy.

Before we plant seeds we dig up the ground. We get rid of any weeds. We rake the soil until it is fine and not lumpy.

Most seeds are sown in rows. That way we can easily keep the rows weeded. We make the rows with a line and a hoe or a stick.

The seeds are sprinkled along the row. Seeds should not be planted too close together or they will not grow properly. Big seeds are planted more deeply than little seeds. Big seeds are also sown further apart.

After the seeds have been planted, the soil is sprinkled over them and pressed down. The seeds are then ready to grow.

24

1   raking the soil
2   making rows with a hoe

3   planting seeds
4   pressing the soil down after planting

Do you remember?

1 What two things do all seeds have inside them?

2 What does the little scar on a seed show?

3 What three things must a seed have to grow?

4 What is the first thing that happens after a seed has been planted?

5 When the skin of a seed splits, what part of the seedling comes out first?

6 What are the tiny hairs on the root for?

7 Where does the stored food inside the seed come from?

8 Name three kinds of food grasses.

9 What is flour made from?

10 Why is grass important for the meat we eat?

11 Why is it best to sow seeds in rows?

12 Why should seeds not be planted too close together?

Things to do

1 **Make a list of the fruits for sale in your local shop.** Find out which countries they come from. You might get some clues from the labels on the boxes.

2 **Make a wall chart or scrapbook of common flowers and vegetables.** Collect pictures from seed catalogs. Cut them out and stick them in your scrapbook or on your chart. Next to each picture, write down the season in which the seed should be planted.

3 **Make a seed necklace.** Collect some dried acorns, walnuts, and other large seeds. Ask your teacher to help you to make holes in the seeds. Thread them on to thin string to make a necklace.

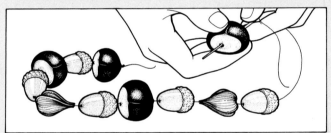

4 **Think about the meaning of these words: fruit, seed, germinate, seed leaves, embryo.** Write a sentence containing each of these words. Look back in the book for some help if you need to.

5 **Each time you eat a fruit, count how many seeds it contains.** Make a chart on which you can write down your findings.

6 **Write a story about an embryo plant.** Pretend you are the plant, warm and snug inside a seed. Describe what happened when your seed was planted and you started to grow.

Experiments to try

7 Measure different kinds of seeds. Do this by putting the seeds between two blocks of wood. Make a chart like the one shown, writing in the kind of seed and how big it is. If you can, weigh the seed.

8 Make some fruit and seed sets. Collect as many different nuts and other dried fruits and seeds as you can find. Draw six large circles on a sheet of paper. Make sets of those fruits and seeds that are round and those that are not round, those that are rough and those that are smooth, and those that float in water and those that sink.

9 Find out about sugar-cane and rice. They are both grasses. Find out all you can about where and how they are grown and how they are used. You could put the information you collect in a notebook.

10 Find out about poisonous plants. Make a list of all the plants you know which have fruits or seeds that are poisonous to humans. How many of these are eaten by birds and other animals?

Do your experiments carefully. Write or draw what you have done and what happens. Say what you have learned. Compare your findings with those of your friends.

1 How far do windblown tree seeds travel?

What you need: A chair; winged seeds such as sycamore, maple, and ash; a long tape measure.

What you do: It is best to do this experiment outside. Stand on the chair. Throw up a winged seed. Watch how it comes down. How far does it travel? Do the same with another kind of seed, and another. Which seeds go the furthest?

Cut the wings off the same seeds. Now how far do they go when you throw them up in the air?

2 How far do dandelion seeds travel?

What you need: Some dandelion blowballs; a long tape measure.

What you do: Count how many seeds are in a dandelion blowball. Blow another dandelion blowball. How many blows does it take to blow away all the seeds? How many feet do the seeds travel?

Moisten the parachute of a dandelion seed. Does it float in the air now? What kind of weather would be best for a dandelion plant to scatter its seeds?

3 Planting seed travellers

What you need: Some shallow dishes such as old saucers or coffee jar lids; filter paper, paper towels, or tissues; saran wrap.

What you do: After you have been for a walk across a park or in the yard or country, carefully scrape the mud from your shoes. Line the saucers or coffee jar lids with several layers of wet filter paper, paper towels, or tissues. Sprinkle the mud from your shoes onto the wet paper and wet the mud. Cover the dishes with saran wrap. Keep them in a warm place.

Do any seeds germinate from the mud? Can you transplant any of the seedlings into plant pots of soil to see what kinds of plants they grow into?

4 Which fruits and seeds do birds like best?

What you need: A plank of wood; at least 10 each of 5 or 6 different kinds of fruits or seeds (weed seeds or tree seeds and berries will do); 5 or 6 coffee jar lids, all the same size; a hammer and some small nails.

What you do: Space the jar lids evenly on the plank of wood and nail them down. Put 10 fruits or seeds of one kind in a lid, 10 of another kind in the next lid, and so on. Place the plank outside where the birds are used to feeding (put out breadcrumbs several days beforehand). Watch carefully and see which kinds of birds come to the fruits and seeds.

Which kinds of fruits or seeds do the birds like best? Do all birds like the same kinds of fruits or seeds?

5 How do grass and cress seeds grow?

What you need: Some empty egg shells; cotton-wool; grass seeds; cress seeds; some clay; a jam jar.

What you do: Take a small lump of clay Gently push the unbroken end of a clean eggshell into it. On the outside of the eggshell draw or paint a face. Fill the eggshell with cotton wool. Wet the wool with cold water. Sprinkle grass seeds on the wet cotton wool. Stand your egg man on a windowsill. Water him carefully every day. Wait for the egg man's hair to grow? How long does it take? What color is his hair?

Make another eggman. Do not give him any water. Does his hair grow? Why?

Keep another eggman in a dark cupboard. Water him every day. Does his hair grow? How long does it take? What color is his hair? Why?

Make another eggman. Keep him in a refrigerator. Does his hair grow? Why?

Make another eggman. Keep him at the bottom of a jar of water. Does his hair grow? Why?

Plant cress seeds to make a new eggman. Water him every day. Does his hair grow? How long does it take? How is his hair different from the grass seed man's hair?

Why do you think that the grass seeds and cress seeds did not grow in the packet you bought them in?

6 Growing seedlings

What you need: Pea seeds, broad bean or runner bean seeds, radish seeds; a jam jar; some blotting paper; a magnifying glass; a knife.

What you do: Soak the seeds overnight in cold water. Cut one seed of each kind open and look for the seed leaves. Look for the embryo plant with a magnifying glass. You may not need a knife to cut the seeds open. You can probably open them with your finger nails.

Fit a piece of blotting paper around the inside of the clean jam jar. Slip one seed of each kind between the filter paper and the glass. Carefully pour cold water into the jar until it is 1 or 1½ inches deep. Stand your jar on a warm, sunny windowsill or shelf. Add water to the jar from time to time so that the seeds never dry up.

Make a table like the one below. Write down the dates when different things happened to your seeds.

Date on which:	Pea seed	Radish seed	Broad bean seed	Runner bean seed
the seeds were planted				
the root shows clearly				
the shoot shows clearly				
the root is about ¾ inch				
the root is about 1½ inch				
the shoot is about ¾ inch				
the shoot is about 1½ inch				
the first leaves show clearly				
the first leaves are really green				
tiny hairs appear on the root				
new roots grow out of the first root				

7 Measuring seedlings

What you need: Broad bean, runner bean or pea seed; a plant pot; some soil; a thin stick.

What you do: Put the soil in the plant pot. Plant a seed in the soil. Put a thin stick in the soil next to the seed. Put the pot where it is warm and light. Give the seed a little water every day.

When the shoot of the seedling appears above ground, measure it and write down the date and the measurement. Measure the seedling every two or three days. Write down the date and measurement each time. As the seedling gets bigger, tie it loosely to the stick with wool for support. Make a graph to show how your seedling has grown.

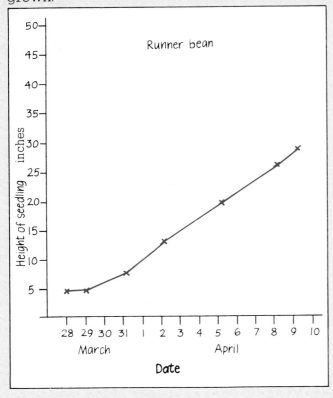

8 Light and cress seeds

What you need: 3 small dishes (coffee jar lids will do); some cress seeds; some blotting paper, tissues or paper towels; 2 small cardboard boxes; scissors.

What you do: Line each of the small dishes with several layers of blotting paper, tissues or paper towels. Wet the inside of each dish. Sprinkle cress seeds in each one. Stand all three dishes on a light shelf or windowsill. Do not let the seeds dry out.

Leave one dish uncovered all the time. Cover another dish with a cardboard box so that the seeds are always in the dark, except for the short time it takes to water them. Cut a small hole, about 1 inch across, in one of the sides of the other cardboard box. Place this over the third dish of seeds. Make sure that the hole is always in the same position when you replace the box after watering the seeds.

What happens to each of these three dishes of seeds? What does this experiment teach you about light and cress seeds? Leave the seeds which were under the boxes uncovered for a few days. What happens?

Try this experiment with other kinds of seeds. Grass seeds, oats, wheat or barley might be good ones to use. They are small and can be obtained in large numbers.

9 Do roots always grow down and shoots grow up?

What you need: A jam jar; some blotting paper; 5 or 6 broad bean or runner bean seeds.

What you do: Soak the seeds in cold water overnight. Put the piece of blotting paper around the inside of the jam jar. Put the bean seeds in different positions between the blotting paper and the jar. Add about an inch of water to the bottom of the jar.

When the bean seedlings have grown roots and shoots look at them carefully. Draw each bean seedling to show which way the root and shoot are growing.

Gently turn one or two of the seedlings upside down. The shoot should then be pointing downwards and the root upwards. Try not to disturb the other seedlings. Watch the seedlings growing for a few more days. Say what happens to them. What have you learned about roots and shoots?

10   Growing tree seeds

This experiment is best started in September or October.

What you need: Acorns, horse chestnuts (conkers), sycamore fruits, hazel nuts, ash fruits or any other tree fruits or seeds; some plant pots; soil.

What you do: Soak the seeds overnight. Plant at least one seed of each kind in a pot of soil indoors, and at least one seed of each kind outdoors. Plant the seeds outdoors either in a flower bed or in pots of soil. Keep the seeds well watered. It may take a long time before all the seeds start to grow.

Keep a record of when the seeds were sown. Make a table like the one below to compare how the different seeds grow.

Do the seeds planted indoors germinate quicker than those sown outdoors? Why do you think that not all of the seeds grow? Do the experiment again, but plant a large number of seeds of one kind in each pot. What happens? How do the seedlings differ from those which were not crowded?

Kind of seed	How many seeds sown?	How many seeds germinated?	Date first shoot appeared	Date first green leaves unfolded
Oak (sown indoors)				
Oak (sown outdoors)				
Conker (sown indoors)				
Conker (sown outdoors)				
Ash (sown indoors)				
Ash (sown outdoors)				

Glossary

Here are the meanings of some words which you may have met for the first time in this book.

Carbon dioxide: a gas in the air that is used by plants to make their food.

Carpel: the part of a flower that grows into a fruit and in which the seeds develop.

Cereals: the food grasses such as wheat, oats, barley, and corn.

Embryo: the tiny plant within a seed.

Fruit: the ripe carpel of a flower that contains the seeds.

Germinate: when a seed starts to grow and produce a new plant.

Grain: the seeds of cereals such as wheat, oats, barley, rice, and corn.

Mineral salts: the chemical substances that plants obtain from the soil and use as food.

Oxygen: a gas in the air; plants and animals use this gas for breathing.

Petal: the part of a flower that is often brightly colored.

Pollen: the yellow dust made by the stamens of a flower.

Seed: the small object within a fruit that will grow into a new plant.

Sepal: the small leaves on the outside of a flower that protected it while it was a young bud.

Stamen: the part of the flower that makes the yellow dust-like pollen.

Acknowledgments

The publishers would like to thank the following for permission to reproduce transparencies:

C Alexander: p. 15 (top), p. 24 (right) and back cover; Bruce Coleman Ltd: J Burton p. 9 (centre) and (bottom), E Crichton p. 23 (bottom), P Hinchcliffe p. 9 (top), C Molyneux p. 23 (top), A Nelki p. 15 (centre) and p. 24 (left), and T Wood p. 10 and front cover; Massey-Ferguson: p. 19 and p. 22 (top); T Jennings: p. 14; A Souster: p. 5, p. 7, p. 15 (bottom) and p. 18.

Illustrations by Karen Daws, Judith Dunkley, Lura Mason and John Wilkinson.

Index